Easter

Parades, Chocolates, and Celebration

Elaine Landau

Enslow Publishers, Inc.

40 Industrial Road   PO Box 38
Box 398   Aldershot
Berkeley Heights, NJ 07922   Hants GU12 6BP
USA   UK

http://www.enslow.com

For Marion Blessing, Director of Religious Education, St. John Neumann's Catholic Church, With thanks and love for her unending help

Copyright © 2004 by Elaine Landau.

Library of Congress Cataloging-in-Publication Data

Landau, Elaine.
   Easter : parades, chocolates, and celebration / Elaine Landau.
    v. cm. — (Finding out about holidays)
   Includes bibliographical references and index.
   Contents: Was that the Easter Bunny? — It started this way — A holiday that is more than a day — Easter symbols — Celebrating Easter — Still more celebrations!
   ISBN-10: 0-7660-2172-6
   1. Easter—Juvenile literature. [1. Easter. 2. Holidays.] I. Title. II. Series.
   GT4935.L36 2004
   394.2667—dc22
                                        2003027483

ISBN-13: 978-0-7660-2172-3

Printed in the United States of America

10 9 8 7 6 5 4 3

To Our Readers: We have done our best to make sure that all Internet addresses in this book were active and appropriate when we went to press. However, the author and publisher have no control over and assume no liability for the material available on those Internet sites or on other Web sites they may link to. Any comments or suggestions can be sent by e-mail to comments@enslow.com or to the address on the back cover.

Photo Credits: AP Photos, pp. 20 (bottom), 26, 32, 36, 40; © 1996–2003 ArtToday, Inc., pp. 6 (top), 11, 12, 14, 15, 18 (inset), 21, 22, 24 (top and bottom), 25 (bottom), 29 (top and bottom), 34 (top and bottom), 35 (bottom), 37; © 1999 Artville, LLC., p. 10; Cheryl Bavaro, pp. 42 (bottom), 43 (top and bottom); Corel Corporation, pp. 7, 8, 9, 13, 16, 17, 18 (background), 19, 20 (top), 25 (top), 27, 28, 30 (top), 38, 41, 42 (top and background), 43 (background), 47; Enslow Publishers, Inc., p. 23; Hemera Technologies, Inc. 1997–2000, pp. 1, 2, 3, 5, 6 (bottom), 30 (bottom), 31 (all), 35 (top), 39, 44, 45, 46, 48; Courtesy of James and Mary Morgan, p. 4.

Cover Photo: © 1996–2002 ArtToday, Inc.; Inset #1, © 1996–2003 ArtToday, Inc.; Inset #2, © 1996–2003 ArtToday, Inc.; Inset #3, © Corel Corporation.

CONTENTS

Many children get their pictures taken with the Easter Bunny during the Easter holiday.

CHAPTER 1

Was That the Easter Bunny?

It is nearly spring. You are at the mall with your family. You do not see it coming. Then you look up and there it is. A large, white, furry rabbit is headed your way. This bunny must be about six feet tall. It is wearing blue overalls and cowboy boots. The rabbit carries a basket of brightly colored eggs. It gives out jelly beans and small chocolate bunnies to children passing by.

Everyone knows the rabbit is not real. Everyone who is older than three, that is. It is a person in a costume. But it is not a Halloween costume. The person in the rabbit suit is

THE EASTER BUNNY

Bunnies are a symbol of spring. There is an old German story about the Easter Bunny. In the story, a woman hid colorful Easter eggs outdoors. Her children went out to hunt for them. Just then, a rabbit hopped by. The children thought the rabbit brought the eggs. After that, parents began telling their children the story. They said that every year the Easter Bunny brings beautiful colored eggs.

The Easter Bunny is one way to tell that Easter is almost here.

pretending to be the Easter Bunny. You see lots of Easter Bunnies this time of year. It is a sign that Easter is almost here.

Easter is a special festival. It is a time for hope and rejoicing. Many children are given Easter baskets filled with treats. They go on Easter egg hunts. Families come together. They enjoy wonderful Easter dinners.

Easter is also a religious holiday. It is a very important day for Christians. Christians believe that Jesus is the son of God. They also believe that after Jesus died, he came back to life. This is known as the Resurrection.

Christians believe that Jesus gave his followers hope. On Easter, Christians celebrate Jesus' Resurrection. They also celebrate the promise of being with Jesus forever in Heaven.

Christians have celebrated Easter since early times. It is the oldest Christian festival. It is the most important, as well. This is a book about Easter and how people make that holiday special.

Easter is a religious holiday celebrated by Christians.

Easter is a spring festival. Flowers and trees start to bloom.

CHAPTER 2

It Started This Way . . .

Easter is a spring festival. Signs of new life are everywhere. Winter's cold dark days are gone. Green grass and spring flowers sprout. Birds that went south for the winter are back. You can hear them singing in the trees.

Today people celebrate Easter because of Jesus. Jesus lived over two thousand years ago. He was a Jew from the area now known as Israel.

Some people thought Jesus was God's son. When Jesus grew up, he preached to many people. He tried to teach them how to live.

A NEW SEASON

We are not sure where the word Easter comes from, but it may be connected to spring festivals. Many years ago, people prayed to a spring goddess. Her name was Eastre. Other people say there was a spring festival called Eastre. Still others claim that the name comes from the German word eostarun, which means "dawn." Dawn is the start of a new day. Easter marks the start of a new season. It is the season of new growth.

9

Jesus lived over two thousand years ago in Israel. This is how Israel looks today.

Some said that Jesus healed the sick. They said he also performed miracles.

Many people began to believe in Jesus. But he had twelve special followers. These were known as the Apostles. They helped Jesus tell people about what he believed.

In time, more people heard about Jesus. Crowds gathered wherever he went.

People waved palm fronds and cheered when Jesus went by.

These people loved and respected Jesus. For years, they had waited for God to send someone to save them. They believed that it was Jesus. They thought of him as a messiah or king.

On a day we now know as Palm Sunday, Jesus came to the city of Jerusalem. He rode in on a donkey. The people cheered as Jesus passed. They waved palm branches to greet him. This was usually done to welcome kings and queens.

By then, many people looked up to Jesus. But not everyone was happy about this. Some

Some Romans did not like Jesus. They arrested him and found him guilty.

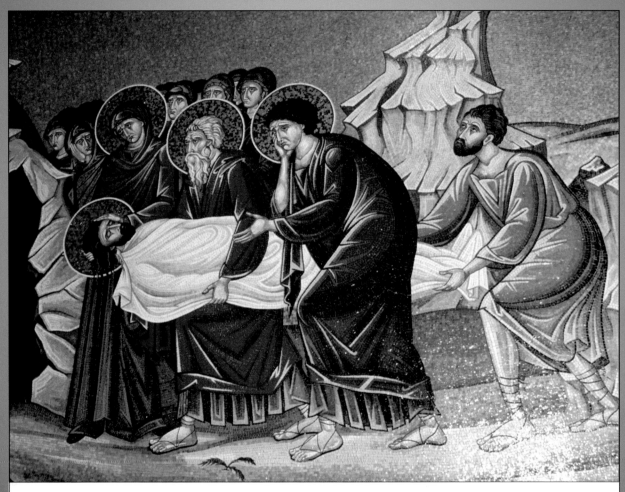

Jesus' followers carried his body to a tomb.

Jesus' followers prayed at his tomb.

thought that Jesus was becoming too powerful. This was especially true of the Romans who ruled then.

While in Jerusalem, Jesus celebrated the Jewish festival of Passover. He ate the Passover supper with the Apostles. Later, he led them to a large garden outside the city. They were to spend the night there. But just before morning, the Roman soldiers came. They arrested Jesus.

A hearing was held. The Romans accused Jesus of speaking against them. They said he had broken their laws. Jesus was found guilty and sentenced to die.

The next day, the Romans nailed Jesus to a

cross. At that time, many people were killed that way.

Jesus died on the cross later that day. But his body was not left there. Before sundown, some of Jesus' followers came. They carried his body to a stone tomb and placed it inside. Then they rolled a large stone in front of it to cover the opening.

Two days passed. On the morning of the third day, some of Jesus' followers went back to the tomb. The stone had been rolled away. Jesus' body was gone.

Jesus' followers remembered what he had told them. Jesus said that he would rise from the dead. Christians celebrate the Resurrection of Jesus as the day on which they believe he came back to life and left his tomb.

Three days after Jesus was buried, he rose from the dead and appeared before his disciples.

Today, sunrise services are held all over the world, as on the Mount of Olives in Israel.

During the next forty days, Jesus was seen again. He appeared before his disciples. He told them to go out and spread the word. They did as Jesus asked. That is how the Christian religion began. Today there are Christians around the world.

Christians celebrate Easter every spring. But unlike Christmas, Easter is not always on the same date. Easter may fall on any Sunday between March 22 and April 25. Whatever the date, Christians celebrate. It is a day to rejoice.

Jesus rode in to Jerusalem on a donkey on a day we now know as Palm Sunday. During the first day of Holy Week, Palm Sunday is celebrated. Some churches give out palm fronds to remind people what happened on Palm Sunday.

A Holiday That Is More Than a Day

Lent lasts for forty days. During Lent, Christians prepare for Easter. They think about their sins. They seek forgiveness. Years ago, Christians did this by fasting. Fasting means not eating or eating very little. For hundreds of years, Christians gave up meat, eggs, cheese, and butter during Lent. Today Christians often give up one thing they really like.

Some holidays only last a day. But Easter is more than Easter Sunday. There is also an Easter season.

The first part of this season is Lent. Holy Week is the last week of Lent. Many churches have special services all seven days. Holy Week reminds Christians of the week of Jesus' death and Resurrection.

The first day of Holy Week is Palm Sunday. Palm Sunday celebrates Jesus' ride into Jerusalem. People waved palm branches to greet him. Today some churches give out palm fronds

Palm Sunday is the first day of Holy Week. Some churches give out palm fronds.

This boy has a dab of ash placed on his forehead at the beginning of Lent.

on Palm Sunday. Often the fronds are made into the shape of a cross.

Lent always begins on a Wednesday. This is known as Ash Wednesday. Large numbers of Christians go to church on Ash Wednesday. Some have a dab of ash placed on their foreheads. This is to remind them to begin Lent with a humble spirit.

Another important day during Holy Week is Maundy Thursday. It is also known as Holy Thursday. That night, Jesus and his Apostles shared the Passover supper. The dinner has become known as the Last Supper. That is because it was Jesus' last meal.

The Friday of Holy Week is called Good Friday. Jesus died on the cross that day.

It is a sad time. Some churches hold three-hour services on Good Friday. There are sermons about Jesus' last words on the cross.

Easter Sunday is the last day of Holy Week. Christians celebrate Jesus' Resurrection. In early times people believed the Easter sunrise was special. They thought the sun danced up to the sky that morning. They would gather outdoors to see it.

Today many churches have Easter sunrise services. The early light reminds Christians of Jesus. They call Jesus "the light of the world."

There are many paintings of the Last Supper. Leonardo da Vinci painted this painting called *The Last Supper* (above). This was Jesus' last meal with his Apostles.

Easter eggs can be decorated in many ways. Some can be fancy and others can be colorful.

CHAPTER 4

Easter Symbols

There are many Easter symbols. A symbol is something that stands for something else. Colored eggs and bunnies are two well-known Easter symbols. We expect to see these at Easter. The holiday would not seem complete without them.

But some Easter symbols were used even before Easter. They were used in spring festivals. Over time, parts of these festivals became mixed with Easter celebrations. So today we think of them as Easter symbols.

HOT CROSS BUNS

Hot cross buns have a cross on top made of white icing. Hot cross buns were made for years before Easter. But they became an Easter symbol. In early times, people thought these buns brought good luck. They would hang a hot cross bun from their ceiling to protect their home. Sailors often took these buns out to sea with them. They hoped the buns would keep them safe during storms at sea.

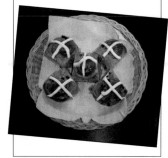

23

Eggs are a symbol of new life. Today, many children and their families decorate eggs.

Easter lilies are pretty plants with white flowers.

EASTER EGGS

The egg is a symbol of new life. For thousands of years, eggs were part of many spring festivals. People would color eggs. They would give these to one another.

EASTER LILIES

Easter lilies are tall, sweet-smelling plants. They have large white blossoms that are shaped like trumpets. The Easter lily is an Easter symbol because of its trumpet like flowers. They stand for trumpets to announce Jesus' Resurrection. The Easter lily's white color stands for purity.

LAMB

For thousands of years, lambs were killed or sacrificed for the gods. They were used as an offering or gift. At Easter, the lamb stands for Jesus. Christians sometimes call Jesus "the lamb of God." They believe that Jesus sacrificed himself on the cross. He did this so God would forgive the sins of the world.

CANDLES

Candles are lit during Easter. Their flame stands for Jesus' light. Light is also a symbol of hope and new life.

EASTER COLORS

Some colors make us think of Easter. These are usually white, yellow, purple, and green. White stands for purity. Yellow is for sunlight. It also stands for the light Jesus brought to the world. Purple is the color of mourning. It stands for the sorrow felt over Jesus' death. Green is the color of nature. It stands for spring and rebirth.

Lambs are a symbol of Easter.

Candles are lit during Easter to stand for hope and new life.

People gather on a beach in Florida for an Easter sunrise service.

CHAPTER 5

Celebrating Easter

Easter Sunday is a time of joy. It is also a day to celebrate. Many Christians go to church that day. On Easter morning, church bells ring out across the nation. Churches are often decorated for Easter. They may be filled with Easter lilies.

People usually look their best. Many adults and children wear new clothes on Easter. Women and girls may have fancy hats. These are sometimes called Easter bonnets.

At times, Christians go to Easter sunrise services. Sunrise services are usually held outdoors. Some are in parks or on beaches.

Others are on hilltops. People get together where they feel close to God. As the sun comes up, they pray and sing. They listen to sermons. Afterwards some groups have a special Easter breakfast.

Other people plan a large Easter meal later in the day. Often it is a wonderful feast. Lamb or ham is served. There may be mint jelly,

Some people plan a large feast for Easter. For dessert they may have delicious cakes.

potatoes, candied carrots, and a wide choice of salads. A white cake baked in the shape of a lamb is a popular Easter dessert. Children are also given Easter cookies. These may be shaped like lambs, bunnies, or angels.

Many Christian families try to be together on Easter. They want to spend this special day with their relatives. Some people travel hundreds of miles to do this.

But Easter is especially wonderful for children. In some families, young people receive Easter baskets. These are baskets filled with treats. Most have lots of candy. Every Easter 60 million chocolate rabbits are eaten. So are over 600 million small marshmallow chicks. Marshmallow eggs and bunnies are popular Easter sweets as well.

There are many ways families can celebrate Easter. This family is taking a hayride to their Easter egg hunt.

Jelly beans are still another favorite Easter

Jelly beans are a popular Easter candy. They come in many colors and flavors.

candy. These are sometimes called jelly eggs. They look like tiny Easter eggs. Americans eat about 15 million jelly beans every Easter. What if all these jelly beans were placed end to end? They could circle Earth three times!

Easter baskets can have more than candy. Some have both small toys and candy. Others may be based on a child's interests. An Easter basket can have just baseball cards and a baseball in it. Another may be filled with art supplies. But one thing is certain. An Easter basket is always a welcome gift.

Some people receive Easter baskets with eggs, chocolate, and other treats.

This fancy egg is a part of the famous Fabergé egg collection. Some of these eggs can be seen in museums.

CHAPTER 6

Still More Celebrations!

People celebrate Easter in many different ways. Stores decorate for Easter. Libraries display Easter books. Sometimes someone in a bunny suit even stops by.

Museums display solid gold Easter eggs. Some are decorated with brightly colored jewels. These can be worth millions of dollars!

Most schools share in the holiday fun. Children decorate their classrooms for Easter. There may be special holiday craft programs. Students make Easter baskets out of cardboard, paint, and ribbons. They make small bunnies out of marshmallows and toothpicks.

Botanical gardens are places where special plants are grown and cared for. Visitors come to see the rare and often beautiful plants there. Every Easter, many gardens have children's activities. The young people may be given seeds to plant in pots. At home, they water and watch over their plants. Soon the plants begin to grow. It is a wonderful way to celebrate both Easter and spring.

Some people make their own cards on Easter. It is a lot of fun!

You can make your own basket with your family.

Students also make Easter cards. They give these to their friends, teachers, and families. Easter cards are the second most common cards sent by young people. Only Valentine's Day cards outnumber them!

Some schools close on Good Friday. Schools may be closed on Easter Monday as well. That is the Monday after Easter Sunday. In many places, there is also no school either the week before or after Easter. This is known as Spring Break.

There are lots of things to do. Before Easter many children like to color Easter eggs. Sometimes families do this together. Friends dye eggs together, too. Some Easter eggs are beautiful. They have fancy designs. Several colors may be used as well. At times, people hang their nicest eggs on the branches of small trees. These are indoor trees. People also hang large plastic eggs on outdoor trees.

Easter eggs are used in other fun ways, too. Both Easter egg hunts and Easter egg rolls are common in the United States. In an Easter egg hunt, children try to find hidden Easter eggs. An Easter egg roll is a bit different. Children roll eggs down a small hill. The child whose egg reaches the bottom first is the winner.

Perhaps the best known Easter egg hunt and egg roll take place in Washington, D.C. These are held on the White House South Lawn. The president of the United States

Two fun things to do on Easter is to color eggs and then go on an Easter egg hunt.

lives in the White House. But quite a few young Americans visit for the Easter activities.

Special guests from other lands are there, too. They tell how Easter is celebrated in their countries. Visitors may also get to see the White House egg collection. It is made up of eggs decorated by American artists. There is one egg from an artist from each of the fifty states.

On the lawn of the White House, children hunt and roll Easter eggs.

Easter egg hunts are also held in other areas. Students at the Blind Children's Learning Center in Los Angeles, California, have a special one. At that hunt, tiny beepers are placed in plastic eggs. These give off a small beeping sound. Children who are blind or do not see very well use their ears instead of their eyes to find the eggs.

The Easter holiday is also well known for parades. One of the most famous Easter parades is in New York City. It takes place every Easter Sunday.

New York City's Easter parade began many years ago. Then people strolled down Fifth Avenue after church. They were dressed in their best Easter clothes. Women wore fabulous hats. It was really a fashion parade.

Plastic eggs can be fun to find. Tiny beepers are placed in eggs like these for blind children to find at the Blind Children's Learning Center in Los Angeles, California.

Many towns and cities have parades on Easter Sunday. Some people dress up like the Easter Bunny.

Today the parade is no longer about fashion. Instead it is a wild and wacky parade. People wear funny hats and crazy costumes.

Disney World in Orlando, Florida, has another famous Easter parade. There Mr. and Mrs. Easter Bunny arrive in a fancy coach. Mickey and Minnie Mouse are in the parade too. They wave to the crowd. You do not have to be there to enjoy the fun. This parade is on TV. Millions watch it from home.

Having fun on Easter is great. But there is much more to this holiday. Many people believe it is important to share with others on Easter. Some people in Kirkland, Washington, planned an Easter food drive. Everyone agreed to bring a food item to the Easter Sunday church service.

It is fun to celebrate Easter. Think of other ways people celebrate the season.

They gave the food to a food bank. From there it went to people in need. The goal was to raise a ton of food. It was a worthy holiday goal.

These are just some of the ways people celebrate Easter. You may know of other ways. It is easy to enjoy Easter and have fun. But it is also important to keep the spirit of Easter alive. That means bringing hope and joy to whatever you do on that special holiday.

Celebrate Easter and the spring season by looking for new flowers.

Easter Craft Project

★

Make Your Own Baby Chicks

Make a table decoration for Easter.

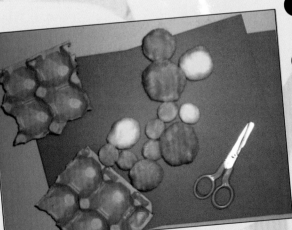

You will need:

✔ **egg carton**

✔ **yellow pom-poms (different sizes)**

✔ **glue**

✔ **orange construction paper**

✔ **scissors**

✔ **markers**

1. Cut the egg cartons in half. Put one half aside.

2. Glue one large pom-pom into each of the six egg holes to form the body of each chick.

3. Glue a smaller pom-pom on top of each large pom-pom. Let dry.

4. Cut six small diamond shapes from the orange construction paper. Fold each diamond in half to make six beaks. Glue them to the front of each small pom-pom. Let dry.

5. Use marker to make eyes on each chick.

Words to Know
★

Apostles—Jesus' twelve followers who helped spread his teachings.

disciple—A person who helps spread the teaching of another.

display—To show.

Eastre—The name of a spring goddess.

fasting—Not eating, or eating very little.

festival—A time of celebration.

hearing—A chance to be heard.

humble—Not bold or proud.

mourning—The sorrow felt over someone's death.

Passover—A holiday that celebrates the Jews' freedom from slavery in Egypt.

The Resurrection—Jesus' return to life after dying on the cross.

Words to Know

★

sacrifice—Something killed as an offering to a god.

sermon—A religious speech by a priest, minister, or rabbi.

sunrise services—Religious services held at sunrise. These are usually outdoors.

symbol—Something that stands for or means something else.

Reading About

★

Chambers, Catherine. *Easter*. Austin, Tex.: Raintree Steck-Vaughn, 1998.

Fisher, Aileen. *The Story of Easter*. New York: HarperCollins, 1997.

Garza, Carmen Lomas. *In My Family*. San Francisco, Calif.: Children's Book Press, 1996.

Hall, Kathy, and Lisa Eisenberg. *Easter Crack-Ups: Knock-Knock Jokes Funny Side Up*. New York: Harperfestival, 2000.

Jackson, Ellen. *The Spring Equinox: Celebrating the Greening of the Earth*. Brookfield, Conn.: Millbrook Press, 2002.

Merrick, Patrick. *Easter Bunnies: Holiday Symbols*. Chanhassan, Minn.: Child's World, 1999.

Potts, Steve. *Easter*. Minneapolis, Minn.: Smart Apple Media, 2001.

Ross, Kathy. *Crafts For Easter*. Brookfield, Conn.: Millbrook Press, 1996.

Winne, Joanne. *Let's Get Ready For Easter*. Danbury, Conn.: Children's Press, 2000.

Internet Addresses

★

CRAFT LIBRARY: EASTER CRAFTS
A website with a lot of crafts ideas
for Easter.
<www.homeschoolzone.com/pp/easter.htm>

CELEBRATE! HOLIDAYS IN THE U.S.A. –
EASTER
A website showing how Easter is celebrated in
the United States.
<http://www.usemb.se/Holidays/celebrate/
eastera.html>

Index

★